T0062999

The Druid Boy

GEMMA KEATLEY & RUTH KEATLEY

BALBOA.
PRESS

A DIVISION OF HAY HOUSE

Balboa Press books may be ordered through booksellers or by contacting:

Balboa Press
A Division of Hay House
1663 Liberty Drive
Bloomington, IN 47403
www.balboapress.com
1 (877) 407-4847

Print information available on the last page.

ISBN: 978-1-4525-2932-5 (sc)
ISBN: 978-1-4525-2933-2 (e)

Balboa Press rev. date: 07/08/2015

Chapter 1

Once upon a time there was a boy who was connected to everything.

He was in tune with every breath that the earth made. He was in tune with the seasons and aware of the weather. He understood the stars. He could communicate with the animals. He did not talk to them, he listened to them. He listened to the wind and knew when the rains were coming. He was at his best when he was within the safety of nature.

He was only six years old, but already he was brimming with a quiet wisdom.

He understood the world and all of the creatures in it, but was confused by only one species, Humans. He loved people dearly but he struggled to understand their thought processes.

Animals were clear in their communication. They acted differently when they were hungry, tired, on heat, protecting or dying.

Humans on the other hand, said one thing and then did the opposite. Humans themselves had no idea what their needs were. They ate when they were sad or tired and they fought with others when they got hungry. They avoided their fertility cycles, and though they feared constantly that they were dying, they had no awareness of when they actually were dying.

Animals followed a regular daily rhythm. They awoke just before the sun came up and went to bed when the sun set. Nocturnal animals did the opposite.

Humans got up whenever they felt like it, and they slept at inconsistent times and for an irregular number of hours.

When the sun went down, they just created new suns in the form of lights, *and* lamps, *and* candles, *and* torches.

The animals used nature to meet their needs and needed very little.

Humans worried that nature would run out, and so they attempted to imitate nature wherever possible. This created more and more waste in the process, and instead of needing very little, humans began to need more and more in order to live. They felt that they were becoming more self-sufficient, but actually they were creating more problems for themselves and others.

The female animals understood their breeding cycles and when it was time to breed they found a partner and created a family. There was always a male of the species ready to fulfil this role, as they too, were in tune with their own breeding cycle.

The humans seemed to be too busy replacing nature, creating work for themselves, or entertaining themselves, to pay attention to their breeding cycle, and when it got in the way of their pursuit for pleasure or career, they created methods to avoid fertility all together.

Later when they decided that they should breed, they used their artificial methods to create their own babies with mixed results.

The animals knew who had fathered their children. Their children were raised by their parents and taught the skills that they needed to survive for themselves.

When humans had their children, due to circumstances they were sometimes unaware of who had fathered them or ended up separated from their fathers. Instead of raising their children with skills for life, humans chose to send them away to schools to be educated with information that was not always relevant or necessary to life and living.

The animals tended to 'go with the flow,' while humans believed it was smarter to 'make their own flow.'

Humans prided themselves on being able to switch nature on and off at will, and with it their bodies and minds as well.

As the human race began to take more and more responsibility for being the gods and creators on Earth and as they began to take on the stress of regulating processes that were already taken care of, they began to get overwhelmed. They began to get irritable, anxious, depressed, and tired. And so they developed pills and tablets to fix these problems.

They developed mental and physical illnesses and tried to fix them with all of their human-made products. They drank, ate, took drugs and hooked themselves into technological devices.

When these human made solutions failed to work, they began to switch themselves off.

This is the world that the druid boy was living in.

Chapter 2

The druid boy had parents, but they were busy. They worked in the human world and they were stressed all of the time.

The druid boy wore glasses. He had to, because all the flashing, bright and artificial lights hurt his eyes. He didn't need his glasses when he was out in nature because his eyes could manage.

The druid boy was given anti-histamines by his parents. He needed them because of his eczema and the allergies that came from the chemicals and preservatives in his human made food.

The druid boy was loved by his parents more than life itself. Anything that he wanted or they thought he needed was provided, and his parents would have given their lives for him, but, it was hard to have time to connect because the human world was so busy.

The druid boy was being abused. If his parents had have known, they would have been horrified, and if they had have known that it was *them* causing the abuse through pure ignorance of what he needed, they would have been devastated.

With the invention of computers and televisions, fast food, mobile phones and social media, the humans had created a frantic new world which made the old world seem completely foreign, but their biology had not caught up with the social changes.

Within a very short time period of only a few generations, humans had created hybrid humans who couldn't survive in either world. The old world was too harsh and the new world was too different. The parents who had been around as the new technologies had emerged had experienced simple childhoods and they saw the changes as exciting and positive. They didn't realise that this new world would deny their children the basics that they had taken for granted, like quality time and relationship development and they didn't realize that is was *the adults* that needed to change and not the children. Some intuitively knew that forcing children to conform to a world that was inherently bad for their physical, mental, emotional and spiritual health was not OK, but they didn't know any other way.

Humans began to create a society that built only for the short term and survived by consuming everything they could get their hands on. They began to produce waste products that they called food and everywhere they went across the planet they changed, altered and destroyed. In the earlier past, people had at least built with quality and longevity in mind, whereas the most recent generations built for novelty and disposability knowing that they would soon tire of everything that was built, made or created.

Some attempted to go back to 'natural' products but even these were tainted. The soil was damaged and the air and water was damaged and often these products were only 'natural' if compared to the current generation's definition, meaning that they may only have 14 chemicals in them rather than the usual fifty plus, if these products had been labeled that way several generations ago, people would have been horrified. It doesn't matter how much you try to convince the world that your candy or chocolate breakfast cereal is 'natural,' it just isn't.

The druid boy needed nature, but he needed it the way it used to be. The soil now was no longer safe to play in and the air was contaminated. The druid boy needed pristine, and yet there was none of that here.

The swimming pools were dirty, the classrooms festering. The animals were shut down from stress. They all sat stagnating in a dying world. But the druid boy had a secret.

HE KNEW HOW TO FIX IT.

Chapter 3

The humans lived as though every minute was their last. Because of this attitude they took no responsibility for the Earth. They ate and drank and turned their whole planet into a rubbish bin.

The druid boy acted as though he would live forever (even though he secretly worried that he wouldn't). He took care of his body and he tried to tidy up after himself.

He considered the Earth to be a living, breathing thing. He knew that the earth would renew itself and he knew to work with her as she did it.

He knew how to read the stars and plot his course accordingly, but he was only little, and grown-ups do not listen to six year olds.

The weight of carrying so much knowledge and responsibility weighed heavily on him and he began to get stressed.

Anxiety began to plague him. He needed the adults to listen and act.

He needed his world to change NOW not next year or even next week.

But how?

The secret was that it wasn't the whole world that needed to change; it was that each individual in it needed to change. Not in big ways, but just in lots of little ways. It was each person's daily habits that were destroying the world and they didn't even realize that these habits could be changed quite easily if they were only aware of them.

The druid boy knew that it was connection that was important. Again this did not have to be at a global level but an individual level. Positive relationships at the level of family and community were all that was needed to tip the balance of emotion into the positive. When individuals got on well with other individuals the greater labelling and generalizations did not need to occur.

When people understood their family values and how to resolve conflict within the family then they had the tools to solve conflict within their greater environment. It was actually the children that had the power to change the world by getting their parents to notice. The world as it was, was not conducive to health on an individual level or a societal level but the change had to come from within each person, not at the group or community level.

But how to get his family's attention?

Chapter 4

He needed his parent to STOP. To question every purchase they made and ask themselves, is there a simpler, healthier choice?

Natural is not always better but a smorgasbord of anything is not healthy.

Too many products, too many options, too many choices had made the humans forget what was important.

SIMPLE, CLEAN LIVING AND GOOD CONNECTION TO YOUR LOVED ONES AND YOUR PURPOSE.

The druid boy did not *talk* to the animals, he *listened* to them.

He did not *make* things grow, he *helped* things to grow.

He *owned* nothing and yet he *had* everything.

He *gave* nothing but he *shared* a lot.

He knew that in a world where we all responded to our callings that there was no competition or fighting. Everyone just did what they were drawn to and as a whole, every job got done.

People were valued and resources that were needed were available.

The druid boy knew all of this but he was running out of time.

Chapter 5

It was pressure that was killing the druid boy. He had a desire to please but he didn't know how to. Everything was too fast and he couldn't keep up.

The druid boy was very intelligent and intuitive but not when he was being timed. Humans seemed to think that the ultimate goal was to make things faster and faster. They never stopped to savour anything and they seemed to think that any problem that could not be solved instantly must require medication.

Humans treated the druid boy in the same way. Instead of sharing in his delightful creative nature, they tut tutted the fact that in school he couldn't keep up. They saw it as a character flaw that he could not eat his lunch as quickly as everyone else, and they were surprised that he did not want to.

The druid boy began to realize that certain foods gave him diarrhoea and that some movies gave him nightmares. The druid boy spent his days trying to keep up with the hyperactive 'normal' kids and when he couldn't please everyone he began to fall apart.

Not that he spoke to anyone else about it initially. He was ashamed at himself for being so weak and sensitive. He knew that he was vulnerable but he didn't trust other people to be able to fix it. Besides, those around him had their own problems.

Each day he was brainwashed by the negativity of every person he met discussing the general stresses of their day. He tried to fix it for them. He offered sympathy, a shoulder rub, soothing words and healing hands but he was shrugged away. No one wanted his particular forms of healing because they were too irritated.

Everywhere he went people seemed to be yelling. They didn't even realize that they were doing it. They all tried desperately to be heard above all of the other voices. Advertising flashed and danced in every possible location. Every wall was plastered with questions such as "Hair thinning?" "Want to satisfy your lady?" "Hungry for a BIG flavour hit?" These were all things that were irrelevant and inappropriate for the young boy to be exposed to, but never the less here they were. Images of scantily clad ladies arrived, advertising underwear in his toy catalogues, and five or six offers a day arrived in his letter box from real estate agents imploring him to sell his house. (He wasn't even aware that he wanted to move!!)

The druid boy didn't know how to manage all of these emotions and so he began to change. He began to let the world in because he was too stressed to block it out. Every ad on the television was met with loud choruses of "I want that! And that!" and the Christmas list was added to daily. When asked what it was that he wanted, most of the time he couldn't say what the item was or what it did but he was sure that he HAD to have one.

When he went on the computer or an iPad the advertising beckoned. Opportunities for accidental clicking were everywhere and again the yelling continued. Children's sites and games were the worst. Parents let their children look at these sites because they advertised that they were specifically for children's learning and development and parents believed the advertising (just as they had been programmed to do). These sites however were simply a platform to reveal to children all of the games, toys and apps that they had to have right now so go and ask, sorry, tell your parents that this is what you need.

Social media was just as difficult. The grownups put family photos up for everyone to share and made commentary on every funny thing that he had done or said during the day and yet *he* was told that privacy was important and to be wary of strangers. He wondered which strangers were sharing the intimate details of his life without his permission. (He became anxious that they would come and steal him while his parents were busy on the computer).

The druid boy observed all that was going on around him wondering why no one else seemed to be doing the same.

Chapter 6

The druid boy watched his parents go through their days. In the mornings they were tired and cranky. This was not something that developed over the course of the day; it was already there before they opened their eyes.

Everything seemed to be something to 'do'. Meals, dressing, driving etc. all seemed to be things to cross off a list. They were the essentials and the necessities. They were not enjoyed for the process or savoured in any way.

Their favourite words seemed to be "hurry up" and "come on, we are going to be late." The druid boy knew that it was important to be on time. He was a very conscientious little boy, but the word was a constant anxiety that hung over his head. Late meant you had failed. Late meant you were not good enough, late meant that you didn't deserve to be in the world and that you had let everyone else down. It seemed that his parents were putting the whole family at risk of these things on multiple occasions every day. No wonder they were all stressed!

Late did not apply just to leaving the house, it was applied to every step in the process. It was possible to be late going to the toilet, eating your breakfast, brushing your teeth, stopping to watch your favourite show, putting on your shoes etc. It seemed that every time the word was mentioned his heart rate went up and his parents looked as though they were running across hot coals.

In all of this rush to avoid being late for everyone else, some very obvious, and some would argue, important, things were regularly overlooked.

Meals were never thought about or prepared ahead of time; they were slapped on the table in the shortest possible time because the kids needed, (sigh) to eat *again*. The most basic of processes seemed to take them by surprise, over and over again.

The druid boy's parents seemed to run on adrenalin most of the time. In the rare instances where they tried to slow down and unwind they just ended up cranky for what they thought was no reason. What they did not realize was that it takes time for the nervous system to settle. They were ready to relax but their body was still playing catch up.

The druid boy's parents argued that they might as well be busy because at least that way, things would get done. It was better than sitting around feeling angry for no reason. They believed that it was the lack of productivity that made them irritable; they did not think that the activities of two weeks ago were still swirling around hormonally within their bodies.

They believed that life had it in for them. When they took a holiday, they got sick. Not just once or occasionally, but every single time. They thought that this was a sign that they were just not meant to relax. Again they failed to realize that their body does not heal itself well when it is in an emergency, it waits until the threat has passed. The druid boy's parents lived in an emergency daily, so it is only when they took the pressure off themselves during holidays, that their body slowed them down and began repairing the systems that had been unavailable previously.

Instead of understanding and supporting this process of regeneration, the druid boy's parents began to dread the holidays or worse still they stopped taking them.

In the druid boy's body, this sort of repair would happen regularly while he slept. His body would do its work and his mind would switch off and he would access his inspiration instead. He would have the most incredible dreams and he would use the ideas that came to him, in his daily life. The results were often astonishing.

The druid boy's parents did not repair overnight as they did not sleep. Of course they closed their eyes and dozed for several hours but during this time their mind did not switch off, it worked overtime sorting through the same garbage that they had thought about during the day. Because they were stuck 'on' during the night, their inspiring dreams that unlocked the answers to their most pressing concerns were few and far between, and when they had them, they were too tired to remember.

The druid boy's parents were deep thinkers but this could be a blessing or a curse. When they were relaxed, these deep thoughts led to the most profound insights, but when they were stressed this sort of thinking led to panic and fear. What needed to change was not the thinking but the state in which they pondered. If the druid boy's parents focused more on relaxing, the answers would have come far more easily.

As well as the essentials even the important things were just a tick in the box so that they could get on with the next job. Things were not pleasant and there would never be any play time for the grown-ups, just a self-imposed never ending to do list.

The grown-ups didn't reward themselves with anything that inspired them. They did not dream anymore because they didn't have time to dream. The only thoughts were ones of escape and switching off. They fantasized about weekends away to ridiculously expensive retreats where they would lounge by the pool and eat and drink and sleep. Fine in theory, but in practice they really couldn't be bothered packing and getting on a plane and they were so in debt that they didn't have the money even if they wanted to. They really didn't feel they had the bodies to be lazing by any pool or beach and really it was just easier to sit on the couch and unwind with a drink the way they always did.

Even conversation was hard with grown-ups. They talked on their terms and only asked what they were interested in i.e. how well each child was fulfilling the expectations that they had set them and mentally adding things to their own 'to do' list as the child spoke.

"How was school today?"

"Good, I played with my friend..."

"Did you do your math test?"

"Yeah, Sarah and I..."

"How did you do?"

"Not sure, I..."

"Hmm I better go and speak to the teacher about that and while I'm at it we really should be going over those spelling lists…"

"Sarah and I played in the sandpit."

"Mm? Oh that's good. I think spaghetti for dinner; I think we have a packet sauce. Hmm maybe not I'd better put that on the list."

The grown-ups would go back to their smart phones and ponder all of the things that now needed to go on the list. Whilst they were at it they would check their email, answer a text to a friend, check out what was happening on the news and update their status on Facebook.

"I'm hungry" the druid boy would say.

"You're always hungry" would come the inevitable reply. His parents would then check the time. "My gosh it's way past dinner time, where on earth does the time go?! Hungry… yes hungry… um. Right, yes, I think spaghetti for dinner; I think we have a packet sauce. Oh that's right I needed to put that on the list…"

Distraction was the staple food supply for these busy people. They forgot to eat, they forgot the basics and they wondered why they needed so much caffeine in order to function.

The druid boy's mother suffered the most as she regularly forgot to eat. She would expend so much energy getting food organized for others but then her own meal would go unprepared or else would sit uneaten in the microwave for most of the day.

It was not that she had a problem with food, just that she existed on a not so helpful binge or forget routine. She either forgot or she ate too much.

She suffered from chronic migraines and though she wracked her brains for a cause or a solution to this debilitating condition she did not realize that it was because she was chronically exhausted and despite being overweight, she was slowly starving herself to death.

It wasn't even a matter of what she ate; it was that her body needed her to eat something, anything on a regular basis.

The druid boy had learnt in school that the human body was made up of more than 70% water and that water was essential for optimum brain and body function. His mother seemed to know this too because every day she packed him a large bottle of water to take to school, and she was always reminding him of how important it was to stay hydrated.

What he couldn't understand then, was why his mother never packed her own drink bottle. He watched in confusion as she began to drink coffee for the first time in the hopes that the caffeine might help her head. She didn't even like coffee. He watched as she went to doctors and specialists and complementary health practitioners. She took tablets and pills and vitamins all over the place, all to seemingly no avail, but what he was bursting to tell her is that if she simply drank a whole glass of water with whatever obscure vitamin she was taking, and had a decent meal at the same time, that her body would have taken care of the problem itself.

Drink water, eat regularly and get some sleep. She didn't need thousands of dollars in specialist fees to solve her problem; she needed to listen to her body.

Chapter 7

The druid boy's parents rarely smiled. He was beginning to see why. Of course when they saw someone at the shop or if they caught up with a friend the smile would go on, but it wasn't a natural, genuine smile, it was a well- practiced out in public smile.

The druid boy's parents thought that it was the kids distracting them but the kids were just desperately trying to reach their parents before they lost them completely.

Because they were otherwise occupied they tended to give their children what they asked for without really thinking about it.

They just became subliminally influenced by their children. The parents were happy to throw away broken toys because there would inevitably be more coming at the next birthday party or fast food restaurant visit. Everything in their child's world became expendable.

When the druid boy broke the trampoline whilst trying to talk to his neighbours more easily, his comment was "Oh well, we'll just have to get a new one". His parents were shocked by his attitude (mainly because trampolines were expensive and they didn't have a spare in the cupboard like they had for most other things), and yet the comment shouldn't have come as a surprise as it was what they had repeated on an almost daily basis, his whole life.

Chapter 8

The druid boy's parents were kind and loving and generous and thoughtful. They followed all of the rules and were doing their best to please everyone, but they were running on empty and by the time they came home to their families they literally had nothing left to give. They had always put themselves last and they seemed to be content to watch their health slipping away because they felt that they were doing what everyone else expected of them.

However, nothing got them fired up more than seeing something wrong with their baby, their sweet little druid boy. They saw their little boy becoming anxious and stressed. He was overloaded and overwhelmed. He was frustrated and not sleeping well. He was teary and frightened. He began to have toileting accidents, refuse to attend school and essentially to give up on himself and the world. The light and joy in his eyes was dimming and finally, they realized that something needed to change.

Chapter 9

And so, one day something wonderful happened. His parents woke up. They rubbed the real world out of their eyes and began to see that something had happened to their happy, loving, charming, responsible little boy. He had lost his sparkle. The world had touched him and the result was not pleasant.

They realized that their lifestyle had to change. They began to work more but in the right areas. His mother finally accepted that being at home with her children, even though she was a highly qualified and proficient professional, was more important than being away from home.

They realized that putting the 'home' back into their house was crucial for all of their wellbeing.

They realized that they had not been eating meals but just foods. They discovered that putting frozen fish in the oven was not cooking, it was just heating. They began to understand how this way of living was impacting on all of them.

His mother acknowledged her intense stress and rather than take a pill or attend therapy, she began to balance her lifestyle. She began to slow her mind by doing all the boring things. She began to take pride in hand washing her dishes and folding the towels. As she actually got her hands dirty around her own home she discovered that she had been holding on to far more than the family ever needed.

She admitted that she had kept even more junk in her mind. She had carried every negative thought that she had ever had and she spent most of her day criticizing herself. Rather than wracking her with more guilt, this insight began to set her free.

She began to tell herself, "I don't need to hold onto this". And she began to let negative thoughts and feelings go.

Funnily enough the slower she moved, the more she achieved, and the more she *felt* she was achieving.

She began to speak to the druid boy as though he was a person. She stopped giving him overwhelming responsibility and gave him permission to be a child. She made a pact with herself to look after her own health and her own family and to stop fretting over the concerns and circumstances of others.

She spoke with the druid boy about his thoughts, his feelings and his dreams. She asked him how things could be different, but she did not expect him to have all of the answers.

She welcomed her children back as a part of the family, rather than as a distraction, and began to appreciate the simple things in life.

Old habits were hard to break and new habits tricky to reinforce, but she persisted, and gradually her health and her sanity returned to her.

She now knew that it was important to keep things simple, rather than speedy, and that establishing her own pace was crucial to feeling calm and relaxed.

She began to observe her behaviour and that of her children. Instead of using her logic to plan things, she felt her routines with her heart. She considered the different pace requirements of her children and planned accordingly.

No longer did she see being fair as giving the same amount to each child. She began to give each child what they needed, when they needed it. For her faster paced children, she provided more active opportunities and for her slower paced children she provided plenty of down time.

She actually began to understand her own rhythms, cycles and moods, and rather than seeing these as weaknesses, she enjoyed working her plans around these genuine needs.

They began to make more money, though they did not do more hours. Their money went further because they were conscious of their spending. They began to spend more money on the good things in life and they could do this because they stopped buying what was irrelevant.

They stopped to take the time to look after what they had, and they no longer had the mentality that everything was disposable.

They aggressively fought their addictions to technology and packed the screens and devices away. They restricted their tech time, and strangely enough after they got over the initial shock of it, they began to find plenty of time in their day to do what they had on their lists AND time to relax and unwind.

The less time they spent online, the less time they desired to be online, and the rest of the world also seemed to manage!

Chapter 10

The druid boy's mother found it both incredibly frustrating and mildly hilarious that she could not seem to concentrate or focus on the most basic task for even five minutes. Her mind wandered, or her body wandered. She found herself starting multiple tasks, but finishing none of them.

When she did manage to get something done from start to finish, she looked around hopefully for someone to hi-five but no one was really that interested. She realized that she had to be her own cheer squad.

In her work she felt relaxed, confident, competent and capable. In her own home she felt overloaded, overwhelmed, helpless, hopeless and totally out of control.

She realized that she sabotaged herself regularly on the grounds of lack of energy, lack of time, lack of motivation, lack of skill or lack of appropriate tools to do each task.

When she gained the motivation, through her druid boy, and she chose to make the time, she realized that she actually could have the energy if she didn't expect miracles. When she actually got the right tools and taught herself the skills she realized that she really could do it.

The work became satisfying and she felt confident and competent in a whole new way.

This was not to say that she wanted to remain in the home for always, but it filled her with a sense of excitement that she could if she wanted to, and that she wouldn't need to feel guilty or less of a person for doing so. She could respect herself regardless of her role or her profession and enjoy her own company in the process.

Chapter 11

The druids boy's mother stopped feeling guilty about asking for help and invited her extended family back in. She had not pushed them away on purpose but had always felt that her children were her responsibility. She felt strongly that being a good parent meant that she should be able to do it all herself, and worried that her family would see it as a burden or a sign that she was not managing if she asked for help.

What she hadn't realized was that her family found her children to be a delight and that they considered it a privilege to spend time with them. They were their family too, after all. She had forgotten that her parents and her in-laws had also raised a family and knew and appreciated how time intensive it could be.

As her children got to mix with their loved ones more regularly, there was a buzz of excitement in the air about where their next great adventure would lead them. Instead of struggling with the idiosyncrasies that the special people in their life had, they fitted in beautifully and adapted well to differences in rules and expectations, and in fact, they were far more adventurous and willing to try new things in these new environments.

During the times that her children were away for an hour or two, the druid boy's mother had a chance to get the basics done, and to have a quiet space to ponder and reflect. She felt inspired during these times and they gave her the opportunity to miss her children. When they returned, they were relaxed, she was relaxed, and she was genuinely excited to chat and hear about their day.

His mother stopped seeing these visits as babysitting and began to consider them for what they really were, family time.

Chapter 12

The more real world adventure her children had, the less they needed their old baby sitter, television, until they almost forgot that it existed. Luckily television was not offended!

The druid boy's parents had been taught that it is important to work hard. They learnt this from their parents who worked even harder. But they had not learnt how to manage their time to include rest.

Before the druid boy was born his parents still saw themselves as busy, but in hindsight, they had had plenty of opportunity for rest, for sleep and for recreation.

When the druid boy came along he *was* the recreation. They looked lovingly at him for hours, they held and cuddled him and poured their love and attention all over him. They found him to be the most fascinating creature in the whole of creation. They shared the same love for their other children too and with this came the need to cut back their attentions in other areas.

They had rightfully let go of the housework as they settled into their new routines, but as the sleep deprivation piled up and their calm, quiet home became the 'play room', they just never really found the time to get it back under control.

Chapter 13

The druid boy's parents initially believed that more toys equaled more opportunities for play, growth and development. They thought that if their children had more and more content and variety, then they would not be plagued by that terrible affliction of boredom.

They loved treating their children to all of the toys that they had when they were children, and all of the toys that they wished they could have had when they were children. But when two grown-ups are playing out their childhood toy fantasies there is bound to be too much and when everyone else in the extended family was playing the same game too, it became plain ridiculous.

When the children began to complain that they were bored, their parents were genuinely bewildered. "Bored?...but how?" They looked at all of the brilliant things that they themselves would have drooled over as children and they were completely at a loss as to how this could be.

They discovered though, that when everything is handed to you and everything is freely given that it is not valued. They also observed that when there is too much to do, it is just as crippling as having nothing to do. They realized that their children too, had come from a long line of hard workers and so they put them to work as a family to clear out the mountain of toys.

They donated, recycled and just plain threw out those things that were not loved and used, and they were even more surprised that their children did not bat an eyelid. There was no outcry of emotion, they were even happy to help. It seemed that the game of spending time with mum and dad and holding a garbage bag was far more interesting than anything they had ever done before.

As the home began to clear of all the unnecessary items and the floors became visible enough to actually vacuum, the children commented that now they had a space to dance, and this was good.

Chapter 14

Their parents cringed at the thousands of dollars and more that they had spent on things that had taken away their children's opportunity for real play, and they considered the type of car they could have bought with the money that they had spent on toy batteries.

As they watched their children play happily together with a wooden train set or a game of snakes and ladders, they had reason to consider their own 'toys'. The druid boy's parents had collected a lot over the years and the reality was that their lives had changed so significantly that their belongings and their furniture no longer represented who they were anymore.

They had not even considered getting rid of these things as they still held onto those beliefs from when they were a child of "This is mine, it is special and I'm keeping it." Only they didn't stop to think that these things actually weren't all that special or all that relevant anymore. Despite thinking that this 'stuff' would remind them of who they were, they had still managed to forget.

They wondered what it would be like if they too could clear some space and have room to dance. They started to fantasize about what they could enjoy if they focused on one or two interests and invested their money into those, rather than having so many of their own toys that they couldn't find the time for any of them.

Chapter 15

They began an experiment. They threw a few things away. Nothing terrible happened. They put a few things out in the garage to see if they missed them. Still OK. They dared to drop off a few boxes of nice things to a charitable organization. Nothing. Strangely they felt better and better with the more that they gave away and this process in itself became more interesting than the things that they were letting go of.

The children thought this was a great game as again they got to hang out with mum and dad and be in charge of big garbage bags.

While they were doing this they would come across sentimental items and have a chance to share their family stories and memories with the children, somehow, allowing the children to witness these memories made it so much easier to let the items go.

The children had fun taking photos of some things as a reminder of what they had but mostly the family enjoyed creating new memories through this process.

This process took time but that was not important. It was all the incidentals, the stories, the laughter, the questions and the reflections that were more important. Finally, this family who had always had so much love for each other were connecting once again.

Chapter 16

The more they shared of themselves with their children and the more they allowed their children to share with them the safer they felt. The druid boy's parents had always worried because he was very sensitive. He was reserved and quiet and liked to watch things first before getting involved.

They had often worried that this would mean that he would miss out on opportunities or fall behind. What they were seeing however, was that they had a very bright boy who understood the subtleties of human nature and was very forgiving.

He asked insightful questions and he took the time to understand and question the answers. He did not rush himself but now, instead of seeing this as a flaw, they began to appreciate that this was an immense asset.

They saw that they had a young boy who would not take risks with his life or the lives of others. That he would learn in great depth and with great reverence, about the things in life that interested him and that if they pushed him just enough to complete his work at school, without the expectation of academic perfection, that he was very easily and naturally capable of being a well-rounded person and successful human being.

Who would have thought that doing more for their little boy actually translated into doing less!

Chapter 17

The druid boy's father went from strength to strength. Because his house was now a home and his wife had woken up, he too began to wake up. He relished his new connection with her and together they rediscovered the love that had attracted them to each other in the first place. He had more energy and less stress. He was relieved that he no longer had to make decisions in areas that he was not comfortable, and felt that he actually had a partner in life.

As a result he felt clearer and more productive in his work, and thoroughly enjoyed his time when he was at home with the family.

He respected his children and his children sought to understand and connect with him.

He was proud of his children for their uniqueness, not because of how well they were doing or managing at school, and he started to see glimmers of their potential now that he had removed his expectations.

When the druid boy told his parents that something was coming and that it was time to move from their home they listened. They made it happen rather than fighting amongst themselves as they would have done in the past. They were no longer emotionally and physically crippled and so when the floods came, they were not affected.

Chapter 18

The druid boy had another secret. He was not here for healing, because there was nothing to be healed. He had come as the healer, to help those he loved the most to stop living in the real world and start living in the new world. A place with less stress, less illness and less pressure. He was actually here to show them how, even if it was initially by staunchly refusing to 'buy' into the relentless human politics and just quietly refuse to play.

He did this subtly and without any form of fight. He was pleasant and respectful and helpful but he would not be shaken or moulded by the world around him. He would not engage in the thoughts that everyone else believed in. He would think deeply but not seek to share these thoughts with everyone around him. He respected the rights of others to believe what they chose to believe.

He would not seek what everyone else sought through the way of traditional 9-5 work and corporate success. Instead he would think differently. He would not expect anyone else to follow him, though in time thousands would.

He very quietly and very pleasantly changed the world just by loving it and the people in it.

The druid boy had started a peaceful and stirring revolution in the world, just by being in it.

The druid boy showed his parents that children have their own systems; they are not a collection of symptoms.

The druid boy and his brothers and sisters still needed to manage their health concerns and allergies while they worked on their environments, but these were no longer the main focus of the family. Health issues were no longer a source of stress, and they were no longer expected to be a permanent feature.

Over time the family began to discover and appreciate that family members choose each other for a reason and that the skills of one complement the alternative skills of another. In a family where everyone contributes according to their own talents and gifts, everything gets done.

The whole family works according to their calling, not their jobs.

The druid boy's family and the families around him began to see the changes and to see the light and glow that now surrounded not only the druid boy but everyone to whom he came into contact. They began to understand his secret of how to 'fix' the world. They began to understand that the earth was returning to the natural order of the world and that this was good.

They began to see that the future was about returning to a time of manners, moderation, modesty and mildness, where success was to be founded and found in the home and in the family, not out on the streets. A time where mothers would be free to be mothers and fathers would be free to be fathers. Where young people would respect their elders and the elders would be worthy of respect. A time where men and women would be valued equally for their roles though their roles may be different.

A time where manners would become the norm and culture would respect those who care for others and nurture others. A time where the children of the world would unite in common goals and a common purpose to reunite the countries and religions of the world.

They began to realize that the world needed to embrace a time when resources would be used appropriately and needs would be met. When wants would be relegated to their natural place down the line from essentials, and others would be able to tell the difference between them.

A time where people would begin to live in the present while always respecting the future.

They saw themselves returning to a time where women would be worth the investment and men would be worthy of authority. When men would lead well and women would manage diligently. When men and women would work hard for and acknowledge their inheritance and strive together to bring harmony to their relationships.

Where women would appreciate men and men would be in awe of the capacity of women, and when all people, men and women alike, would no longer fear growing up.

They became excited about returning to a time when wisdom and maturity would be something to strive for and where sound reasoning would be normal. Where words would be spoken with care and consideration and actions would be benevolent and courteous.

A time when the energy would spark between men and women, inspiring the desire for unity, for oneness and for fidelity and monogamy. A time when relationships would be sacred and valued as a commitment for life.

Those around him finally understood that the world was returning to what life was meant to be in the first place, Paradise.

This is the world that the druid boy had created. Now, when he thought of his family, he smiled.

A letter from the Druid Boy

Dear Mum,

I am an empath. I know how you feel most of the time. When you are angry I feel it. I do not always know why you feel that way so sometimes I assume it is because of me.

The best gift that you can ever give me is to be happy and relaxed. Then I get to share in these feelings too.

Because I know what it is like to feel pain, both physical and emotional, I am careful not to inflict it onto other people. You may describe me as kind, sensitive and gentle.

When I am overloaded and burnt out, which can happen at any age, even as young as six months, I may throw a tantrum, get angry and lash out either physically or emotionally. This is hugely out of character for me and this may shock you so badly that you yell and scream at me. Please do not blame me or be angry with me during these times. Please do not make me feel guilty or go into long detailed spiels about how my behaviour was inappropriate and why. I *know* what I have done was wrong and if you give me twenty minutes to calm down I will soon be making *myself* feel far more guilty than you could ever make me.

When I am really stressed I may regress. In my frustration I may do the unthinkable like wet or dirty my pants. If this happens please realize that this is not me needing constant reminders about how to use the toilet. I am stressed, frustrated, worried or upset.

Hear me without judgement or criticism and the symptoms of my distress will resolve on their own.

I long to please you and I will bend over backwards to try, but please do not take advantage of me. I am happy to help out, but please do not make me responsible for the things that are yours. Please do not make me grow up too quickly just because you know that I can.

Maturity does not mean that I have to forfeit the pleasures of life.

Sometimes my kindness can be a handicap. I wait until last; I give things to others because I can feel in my stomach that they need it more. This doesn't mean that I don't have a great desire for these things myself. I can intuit on behalf of others but this is where I need you to intuit on *my* behalf. This is where I need you to advocate for me.

When I have given up my turn for someone else, push in on *my* behalf and make sure I get my go, even if I then say I don't want a turn. Show me by your actions that you think that I am just as worthy and deserving as every other kid. Sometimes I may say no and sometimes I may say yes but please make sure that you are alert to my needs.

I am not a violent or nasty person but I need to let off steam even more than most. Do not ban me from things that you think will give me nightmares, let me make my own choices and regulate what I desensitize myself too. At the best of times I find my emotions overwhelming and sometimes I just need to switch off too. Computers and technology do not have feelings and I appreciate being able to interact with something that allows me to just be with *my* emotions.

Of course too much time can become addictive, just like most adults are addicted but a bit of time is good for me. Yes mum, even if it make my eyes hurt and the content is not always 'rated G for general viewing!'

You need to know that I love you unconditionally and that I see past the flaws that are inherent in every person.

I know that you are trying your best and I am always able to forgive. I know that you love me and that you feel guilty and worried a lot of the time, but it's OK, and I am OK. If you let go of your guilt and just do your best we will all manage a lot better.

I long to be competent and responsible. Please baby me when I need it, because I need that too, but also let me explore at my own pace. Again, you do not need to be scared for me because I am scared enough for myself without needing to manage your anxiety too.

We know each other well enough for you to let me do what I can, and rely on me to tell you what I can't do. When I ask for help with something and am getting frustrated please help me. You know that I wouldn't be asking unless I needed it, and this is a way that you can show me that you value and respect me.

Most of all, just remember that I love you because you are lovely. There is nothing in this world that we cannot face together and I will always be there for you. If you can be there for me in some of the ways that I have mentioned above then we are in for the most wonderful time!

Much love your Druid Boy.

Reflections on the Druid Boy

The story of the Druid Boy is so relatable because we all know one. We may have parented them, taught them, or we may be one our self.

The name of the book comes as a reference to the Druids, the wisdom bearers of the pagan era. They were all but wiped out with the introduction of other religions but their legacy still exists today.

The druid boys of the world need our assistance and understanding because they have so much to offer but often they are falling through the cracks of society.

They are bright and talented, but they harbour anxieties, they get overwhelmed and they may feel hopeless about their ability to 'fit in' with 'normal' less sensitive others.

They question and think a lot and they know a lot about human behaviour because they tend to listen and reflect rather than speak and act.

Druid boys are fiercely competitive but because of their empathy, they find it difficult to compete with anyone face to face. They are more likely to spend the time apologizing for winning or helping the other person to win because that would be the fair thing to do.

They often feel that fair is a major guiding principal, however, they do not always factor their own right to fairness into the equation.

Druid boys benefit greatly from being able to perfect a skill competing against their own personal best, or alternatively they do very well competing on line against people that they can't see or don't know. This distancing from the emotions of others helps them to put their own feelings first and allows them to develop their skills without someone else watching them.

The druid boys love stories. They connect very well with the emotions of others (when they are not being overloaded with them). So getting them interested at an academic level is often about giving the concepts that they are learning about, faces and stories.

This works in math by drawing out the concept in the form of a story. For example, even numbers are the nice fair ones that can be shared between you and a friend. Usually it's what the druid boy puts in his pocket when he goes out to play with a friend. Two toys cars, four lollies, etc.

Odd numbers are useful because once you have shared them out with a friend you still have a spare left over. It's always helpful to have a spare!

Druid boys need a balance between caring for others and having permission to care for themselves. For example, at the school canteen or tuck shop the druid boy always needs money for two ice creams or a big bag of something so that he can share with others. He will find it very difficult to get it only for himself and if he does he will probably feel sick after eating as he feels subconsciously guilty for not sharing.

The internal world of a druid boy is complex and multilayered.

Druid boys need accommodations in the classroom. They may feel overwhelmed by the sheer number of people around them or the pace of the day and the work. They are generally very intelligent and thoughtful and will want to keep up and please a teacher, but when they are overloaded they may become frustrated and or disengaged. Generally the teacher will have no idea because druid boys tend to be very quiet, polite and well-mannered and get on well with others. Often they suffer in silence until an astute parent or teacher picks up that they are struggling. They need extra time to complete work, particularly tests, and need support and personal encouragement. They often need one on one assistance as they seek to know the work deeply and personally, something which is not always possible in a traditional school environment.

Druid boys make great friends and are very compassionate. They prefer small groups or one on one friendships and are well suited to homeschooling if accommodations cannot be made within the school environment.

Druid boys learn what is necessary and what they love. They have a very practical hands on way of learning and always need to know how something is relevant or fits in with their thoughts and ideas. They love to learn through stories and discussion, although they like the privacy of having their own thoughts and feelings and pondering on them without having to 'prove' that they understood. For this reason, it is often worth reading a story and letting them spontaneously talk about it and then doing a follow up the next day to ask them what they remember of the story and the characters etc. and how it fits in with their life now, rather than expecting them to have the answers straight away.

Druid boys do well in healing professions, both mainstream and complementary therapies and make great counsellors and mentors.

Their love of freedom means that they prefer to be given a task and not micromanaged. Correct them where necessary but encourage their independence. They do better with a to do list for the day to be completed in their own time rather than a schedule, and if they are able to devote time to things that they love doing they will complete a tremendous amount of work and demonstrate vast amounts of detailed, interconnected learning.

In a work environment, druid boys will give it their all. They have a good work ethic and they like to help out, but they may not have the confidence to interview for a position. They are not comfortable selling themselves and they are often far better at telling you why each of the other candidates deserve the job just as much. They may prefer to work their own hours or be employed on a casual basis. This helps them to feel that they are a little more in charge and they can have the quiet time they need to contemplate their own things.

Druid boys love to live the simple life. As adults they love nothing better than sitting out in the back yard with a barbeque, friends and a few drinks. They love quality in what they have but they are happy to survive on very little.

They are quick witted and fun to be around. They are friendly and popular. They are well liked and well respected.

By being aware of your druid boy's personality and sensitivities you can help him to enhance his skills. Druid boys often get lost in the system because they internalize their anxieties.

You are helping your druid boy to listen to his body and respect his natural inclinations. They respond better with less anger and less yelling. There is always a good reason for everything your druid boy does, even if you or he doesn't yet know what it is.

Do not overload your druid boy with too much information, particularly information that is filled with emotional content. They do not need this and it affects their immune systems in a negative way.

It is important though to find a balance, as you cannot protect them from everything or hide things from them. They feel these things too.

Druid boys can suffer from self-esteem issues that we have projected upon them. As parents we are generally sensitive ourselves and we do not give ourselves enough compassion and care. We become angry about the way in which our sensitivities restrict us and we project this onto our children. We do not want them to suffer a similar fate and so we either push them too hard and expect too much from them, or we dont encourage them at all because we think that they are not capable, when, in fact they are.

It is a fine balance between considering what anxieties are yours and what are theirs. Minimize the anxiety that you put onto your druid boy by seeking support and relaxation elsewhere.

Druid boys respond very well to physical affection and so a hug or cuddle when they are upset means far more than you trying to work out what is going on.

Be patient with your druid boy. Although issues may seem urgent, there is always time to calm yourself and then think things through.

Most importantly, do not beat yourself up or feel guilty about the experience that your druid boy has. You are doing the best you can and sometimes the best thing you can do is accept yourself the way you are and be kind to you.

The very best that we can do is to slow our world down. It is spinning far too quickly for all of us to manage and it is up to the grown-ups to do something about this, not for our children to just adapt and spin faster.

Yoga, meditation, breathing, massage and water are all wonderful ways to help druid boys relax and these things work well for grown-ups too.

Letting druid boys access their computers and their technologies helps them to unwind. They need some level of independence with this as it is hard to unwind whilst a grown up stares over your shoulder giving advice or monitoring everything. If you are concerned about security issues or inappropriate content, look into how to block these things or work around them. Discuss these issues with your druid boy and check in with them regularly.

Being lucky enough to have a druid boy in your life means that you will become more and more self- aware. As issues arise you will naturally lean towards self-reflection and in doing so you will learn far more about your own personality and teaching style than if you had not had the pleasure of their influence.

Druid boys are an asset to any family, classroom, workplace or social situation. Their quiet gentle natures, their quick witted humour and warm sociability leave everyone they get to know, feeling good.

Isn't this something that the world could use a little more of?

Printed in the United States
By Bookmasters